STEAM ON T:
ISLE OF WIC

The Postwar Years

Adrian Kennedy

UNIQUE BOOKS

Front cover: Class O2 0-4-4T No W33 *Bembridge* awaits departure from Ryde Pier Head station. The station was significantly modernised by the Southern Railway after the Grouping of 1923 with a fourth platform added and the platform canopies replaced. Although the locomotives based on the island had been painted green under Southern ownership, BR decided to adopt the lined-out plain black livery on secondary passenger locomotives. As a result, although green predominated in the early BR era, gradually all the surviving locomotives were to appear in this style of livery. *Marcus Eavis/Online Transport Archive*

Previous page: No W33 *Bembridge* is pictured again but this time a decade earlier as it is seen at Newport, still in Southern ownership, on 16 April 1946 on an eastbound service. *Tony Wickens/Online Transport Archive*

Steam on the Isle of Wight: The Post-War Years
First published in the United Kingdom by Unique Books 2020

© Text: Author 2020
© Photographs: As credited

ISBN: 978 0 9957493 9 9

A CIP record for this book is available from the British Library

Unique Books is an imprint of Unique Publishing Services Ltd, 3 Merton Court, The Strand, Brighton Marina Village, Brighton BN2 5XY.

www.uniquebooks.pub

Printed in India

A note on the photographs
All of the illustrations in this book have been drawn from the collection of the Online Transport Archive, a UK-registered charity that was set up to accommodate collections put together by transport enthusiasts who wished to see their precious images secured for the long-term. Further information about the archive can be found at:
www.onlinetransportarchive.org
or email secretary@onlinetransportarchive.org

INTRODUCTION

At the Nationalisation of the railways in 1948, British Railways inherited from the Southern Railway the small – but separate – network of lines that served the Isle of Wight. These lines, which had developed from the late 1860s onwards, connected the myriad communities on the island and provided both passenger and, in the era when the railways were still the Common Carrier, freight services.

These services were operated by a small fleet of steam locomotives; Class O2 0-4-4Ts that originated from the London & South Western Railway dominated but there were also two types of ex-London, Brighton & South Coast 0-6-0Ts. The ex-LSWR locomotives had been introduced to the island by the Southern Railway from 1923 onwards as part of the post-Grouping modernisation of the railway. This works also included the expansion and rebuilding of Ryde Pier Head station. During the late 1940s BR increased slightly the number of 'O2s' operational, transferring two additional locomotives to the island in April 1949 in place of the two ex-LBSCR 'Terriers' – Nos W8 *Freshwater* and W13 *Carisbrooke* – that returned to the mainland. The other ex-LBSCR locomotives – the four Class E1s – were to survive until the second half of the 1950s when declining traffic saw them withdrawn.

As elsewhere, the post-war years saw the deterioration in the finances of the railway industry on the island and, from the early 1950s, the network was gradually to succumb. The first casualty was the branch from Merstone to Ventnor West, which was to close completely on 15 September 1952. The following year witnessed the demise of the long branch from Newport to Freshwater and the shorter line from Brading to Bembridge, both of which closed completely on 21 September. The next casualty, on 6 February 1956, saw all traffic withdrawn from the Newport to Sandown via Merstone route. This left two key services: from Cowes to Ryde via Newport and from Ryde south to Ventnor.

By the early 1960s the position of these two routes was becoming increasingly precarious. Both locomotives and rolling stock were becoming increasingly aged whilst freight traffic was in serious decline. In theory it might have proved practical to re-equip the lines with more modern rolling stock – indeed there were plans to transfer Ivatt-designed 2-6-2Ts to the islands – but, due to the restricted loading gauge, any such modernisation would have been costly and, given the decline in traffic, difficult to justify. Unsurprisingly, the Beeching report of March 1963 included the proposed closure of both routes – something that had already been planned – with the intention of retaining only a shuttle along the Pier linked to a new bus station at Esplanade. Inevitably there was opposition – a group entitled the Isle of Wight Railways Restoration Committee had already been created to fight the possible closure of the routes – and an agreement was reached: the Ryde to Shanklin section would be retained and modernised, using second-hand ex-London Underground rolling stock whilst the sections from Smallbrook Junction to Cowes and from Shanklin to Ventnor would be closed.

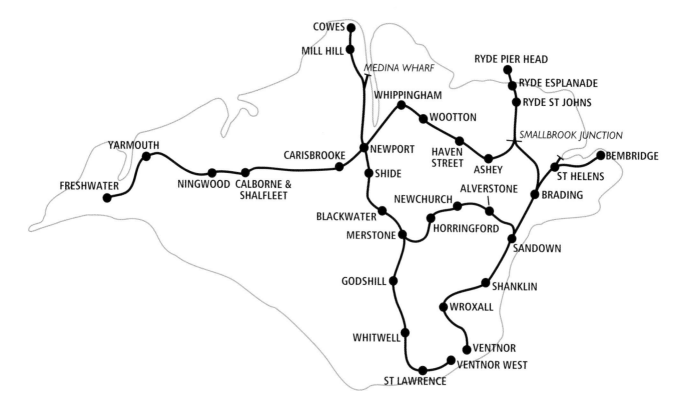

The original planned closure date for these sections – in late 1965 – was delayed, with the result that the Cowes route was to close completely on 21 February 1966 with the Shanklin to Ventnor line following two months later, on 18 April. This meant that for the final season of steam operation only the section from Ryde Pier Head to Shanklin was operational; this still, however, required some 10 locomotives in steam at peak hours. The final steam operated passenger services ran on 31 December 1966 although a couple of the 'O2s' remained active into 1967 in order to assist with the modernisation work.

This was not, however, to be the end of steam operation on the island as a preservation scheme was to be established. Supported by the late David Shepherd No W24 *Calbourne* was secured for preservation along with a number of items of rolling stock. These were initially stored at Newport but, following the acquisition of the lease at Havenstreet, all the stock was relocated there on 24 January 1971 – these workings represented the last steam trains east from Newport. Today, the preserved Isle of Wight Steam Railway runs from Smallbrook Junction – where a new interchange station has been constructed (the first station ever built to serve the junction) – and Wootton.

Above left: The railway network on the Isle of Wight managed to survive intact through until the British Railways era. However, the first closures occurred in the early 1950s. This poster was issued to announce the withdrawal of services on 21 September 1953 from the Bembridge branch and the line from Newport to Freshwater along with two intermediate stations – Wootton and Whippingham – on the line from Newport to Ryde. By the end of the decade, the only lines still operational were those from Cowes to Smallbrook Junction via Newport and from Ryde to Ventnor.
F. E. J. Ward/Online Transport Archive

Above right: Not all closure notices were official; this unofficial version records the fact that the line to Freshwater had survived for 64 years by the time of its closure.
F. E. J. Ward/Online Transport Archive

During 1955 two of the 'O2' class 0-4-4Ts allocated to the Isle of Wight – No W20 *Shanklin* on the left and No W22 *Brading* on the right – await departure from Ryde Pier Head station. The line north from Ryde St John's Road was jointly promoted by the London & South Western and London, Brighton & South Coast railways in order to provide a railway connection to the ferry services that the railways operated across the Solent. Engineered by the LBSCR's chief engineer, Frederick Banister, the line opened on 12 July 1880. Originally provided with three platforms, a fourth was added in 1933. Completed at Nine Elms in March 1892 as LSWR No 211, No W20 was, with No W19, the first of the class to be transferred to the Isle of Wight in 1923. Withdrawn in January 1967, the locomotive was scrapped in May of the same year. No W22 was also built at Nine Elms, in June 1892 as LSWR No 215; it was transferred to the island in 1924 and was one of the class that survived through until the end of steam operation in December 1966. Although all locomotives on the island were numbered in the 'W' series, the prefix was not carried on the buffer beam nor the side of cabs but was used on the number plate carried on the rear of the bunker. *John McCann/Online Transport Archive*

In September 1963 two of the O2' class – Nos W24 *Calbourne* and No W26 *Whitwell* – are pictured at the southern end of Ryde Pier Head station. Both of the locomotives were transferred to the island in 1925 and had originally been LSWR Nos 209 and 210 respectively. Both were built at Nine Elms in December 1891. However, whilst No W26 was withdrawn in May 1966 and scrapped three months later, No W24 was to survive until the final steam workings on the island and was subsequently to be preserved. Based for three years at Newport thereafter, the locomotive was relocated to Havenstreet in January 1971. It is the only member of the 'O2' class to survive in preservation. *Phil Tatt/Online Transport Archive*

With the tracks of the pier tramway in the foreground, No W35 *Freshwater* departs from Ryde Pier Head station. On the right can be seen Ryde Pier Head signalbox; this was located immediately to the north of the scissors crossover that controlled entry and exit to the four platforms situated at the terminus. Following the Grouping in 1923, the Southern Railway undertook a major rebuild of Ryde Pier Head station; this included the creation of the fourth platform road, the installation of new steel canopies and the rebuilding of the original wooden main station building into a much more impressive structure. The original signalbox was retained; this was to survive the electrification of the line, not being finally abolished (along with the final semaphore signals) until 5 May 1974. This work also resulted in the removal of the scissors crossover, with the running lines now signalled for bi-directional running. More recent work has seen the facilities at the station considerably reduced.
F. E. J. Ward/Online Transport Archive

No W30 *Shorwell* heads south from Ryde Pier Head as holidaymakers make their way on foot along the pier. Construction of the first pier at Ryde – that over which the pedestrians are walking – commenced in June 1813 and the original structure – some 576 yards in length – was opened in July 1814. Subsequent extensions have taken this structure to its current length of 745 yards. In 1864 a second pier alongside the original was opened; this accommodated a tramway that linked the pier head via the esplanade to Ryde St John's Road station. Initially horse powered,

between 1886 and 1927 the tramway was electrically powered and from then until closure in 1969 the vehicles were petrol- or diesel-powered. The pier carrying the tramway and be glimpsed between the two main structures; following closure in 1969 this pier was largely dismantled although traces are still visible. The opening of the third pier, which carried the railway extension from Ryde St John's Road, was on 12 July 1880. The extension was promoted by the Portsmouth & Ryde Joint Railway, a subsidiary of the London & South Western and the London, Brighton & South Coast railways.

In March 1950 No W21 *Sandown* departs from Ryde Esplanade with a service towards Ryde Pier Head. In the background can be seen one of the petrol-engined vehicles in use on the standard gauge tramway that ran parallel to the railway to the pier head. As a result of the conversion of the line from electric to petrol operation, the Drewry Car Co supplied two petrol-engined four-wheel railcars for use on the line. The operation of these vehicles, which could accommodate 90 passengers, was odd in that they had a driving cab at only one end and, in the reverse direction, the driver used rear-view mirrors and a countdown marker system to judge the approach to the pier head terminus; this was not always successful and there were a number of incidents where the railcars hit the buffer stops. In the late 1950s the petrol engines were replaced by diesel but, as a result of an inspection in 1968, the service ceased on 26 January 1969. Although No 2 was preserved, its bodywork was removed prior to transport to Newport and stored. The powered chassis was used for shunting operations at Newport before the preserved railway relocated to Havenstreet. Unfortunately, during storage, the bodywork decayed and was subsequently scrapped. In 2015 work started on a project – still to be completed at the time of writing – to construct a replica body on the chassis with work being undertaken by Alan Keef Ltd. *Neil Davenport/Online Transport Archive*

Heading south from the pier, the first station on the island itself is Ryde Esplanade and this view sees W27 *Merstone* departing from the station with a southbound service shortly after Nationalisation. The Pier Head terminus can be seen in the distance. The first station opened here on 29 August 1864 in connection with the horse drawn service that operated along the newly-constructed pier; the horse drawn tramway was extended south to St John's Road in 1871 but was replaced, and the station at Esplanade rebuilt, by the joint LBSCR/LSWR route opened in 1880. No W27 was originally built as LSWR No 184 at Nine Elms Works in June 1890; it was transferred to the Isle of Wight in 1926 and was one of the class that survived through until January 1967. The surviving section of the Isle of Wight network – from Ryde Pier Head through to Ryde St John's – was closed temporarily on 1 January 1967 to facilitate the completion of the electrification work that enabled the replacement ex-London Underground stock to be introduced. The section reopened on 20 March 1967.
D. Kelk/Online Transport Archive

With the Esplanade Hotel and the Southern Vectis buses in the background, No W19 *Osborne* prepares to depart from Ryde Esplanade station in March 1950 with a southbound service. The view shows to good effect the livery worn by the locomotives in the early BR period when the 'Southern' previously borne on the side tanks was replaced by 'British Railways' in a similar style on the Southern malachite green livery. Close examination of the side tank illustrates that a simple strip was repainted and the new lettering applied. Also clearly visible is the enlarged coal bunker that was first introduced in 1932; this had the effect of increasing the coal capacity from 1½ to 3¼ tons, thus permitting the locomotives to operate a full summer Saturdays schedule – some 200 miles – without having to return for recoaling to St John's Road. No W15 was originally LSWR No 206 when completed at Nine Elms in September 1891; transferred to the island in 1923 – one of the first two to make the journey (with No W20 *Shanklin*) – it was also one of the first to be withdrawn (in November 1955). *Neil Davenport/Online Transport Archive*

The proximity of Ryde Esplanade station to Ryde Pier is clearly evident in this view that records No W33 *Bembridge* awaiting departure with a southbound service. Ryde Esplanade was the temporary terminus of the extension from St John's Road between 5 April 1880 and 12 July 1880 when Pier Head station formally opened.
F. E. J Ward/Online Transport Archive

A southbound service behind No W21 *Sandown* has just departed Ryde Esplanade station and is approaching Ryde Esplanade Tunnel as it passes the coach park. This area is still used for coach parking in the 21st century but the modern view now also includes the buildings of the Ryde Hoverport. Constructed as LSWR No 205 at Nine Elms in September 1891, No W21 was transferred to the Isle of Wight in 1924. It was to survive in service until May 1966 when it was withdrawn following the closure of the section from Shanklin to Ventnor on 18 April 1966.
F. E. J. Ward/Online Transport Archive

During September 1963, No W33 *Bembridge* heads southbound as it descends over the 1 in 50 gradient towards the northern portal of the 391-yard long Esplanade Tunnel. The tunnel – effectively a covered way built by the cut-and-cover method – is below high tide level and a pumping station to drain the tunnel was constructed alongside Esplanade station. The reduced loading gauge of the replacement ex-London Underground rolling stock employed after electrification enabled the engineers slightly to raise the tunnel floor in 1967.
Phil Tatt/Online Transport Archive

A southbound service is recorded here having just emerged from Ryde Esplanade tunnel. At this point the double-track section runs parallel to the Monktonmead Brook alongside the Simeon Street Recreation Ground. The next stop will be Ryde St John's Road.
F. E. J. Ward/Online Transport Archive

On 9 September 1963 No W31 *Chale*, one of the class fitted with a Drummond boiler, is seen approaching Ryde St John's Road station from the north; it is about to pass under the road overbridge that carries St John's Hill. No W31 was one of the oldest of the 'O2' class transferred to the island; it was new in April 1890 as LSWR No 180 and was one of two of the class – the other being No W24 *Calbourne* – that survived into March 1967 to work the engineering trains for the final electrification work. Efforts were made to try and secure No W31 for preservation but only No W24 was eventually to survive. The 'O2' class was originally designed by Williams Adams with 60 being constructed at Nine Elms between December 1889 and March 1895. A number were fitted with Drummond-type boilers with Ross safely valves on top of the dome; the modification did not result in a significant improvement in performance and most retained their Adams boilers throughout their life.
John Meredith/Online Transport Archive

On the same day, No W21 *Sandown* stands in Ryde St John's Road station with a southbound service. The station was originally known as Ryde when opened, courtesy of the Isle of Wight (Eastern Section) Railway, on 23 August 1864 when it was the northern terminus of the line from Shanklin. The suffix 'St John's Road' was added on 5 April 1880 when the line to Esplanade was opened. In the background can be seen Ryde Works; the works incorporated the original Isle of Wight (Eastern Section)

locomotive shed, a two-road brick-built structure that opened originally with the line in 1864. It closed a decade later when it was absorbed by the works (part of the 1864 shed can be seen on the extreme right of this photograph); a replacement two-road shed, to the south of the station on the west, was opened in 1874. This was itself replaced by a new shed constructed by the Southern Railway in 1930.
John Meredith/Online Transport Archive

Following the Grouping in 1923, the Southern Railway undertook some considerable investment in the network that it had inherited on the Isle of Wight. The first of the 'O2s' were transferred from the mainland in 1923 and, in 1930, a replacement shed was constructed at St John's Road. The new structure – as seen here in September 1953 with No W28 *Ashey* alongside in September 1953 – was constructed in concrete blocks and asbestos sheeting. The new shed replaced the shed constructed south of St John's Road in 1874 with the latter structure being demolished.
Phil Tatt/Online Transport Archive

Two of the 'O2' class – Nos W24 *Calbourne* and W28 *Ashey* – are pictured outside the third shed to be constructed at Ryde St John's Road. With the contraction of the island's network and the final elimination of steam operation, the 1930-built shed was closed on 31 December 1966 and was subsequently demolished.
F. E. J. Ward/Online Transport Archive

Towards the end of the station's life – it closed on 21 September 1953 – an eastbound train awaits departure from Whippingham station behind No W25 *Godshill*. The station here opened with the line on 20 December 1875. The second platform and passing loop were added in 1912. The loop was abolished in 1956 with the line through the eastbound platform lifted. Passenger services over the line ceased on 21 February 1966 although freight traffic continued west from Smallbrook Junction to Medina Wharf until October 1966. The last train east from Newport operated on 21 January 1966 when No W24 *Calbourne* hauled six coaches and assorted wagons from Newport to Havenstreet as the Isle of Wight Locomotive Society transferred its operations eastwards. *Julian Thompson/Online Transport Archive*

In September 1963 a service from the Cowes line approaches Smallbrook Junction from the west prior to heading northwards to Ryde. A junction was created here following the opening of the Ryde & Newport Railway – a line authorised on 25 July 1872 – on 20 December 1875. Initially there was no physical junction at Smallbrook; two separate single lines were operated into Ryde, each operated by one of the two companies that served the town. Following the Grouping in 1923, the Southern Railway invested in improvements to the island's railway network; in addition to the transfer of replacement locomotives – the first of the Class O2 0-4-4Ts – the work included the creation of a physical junction at Smallbrook. Although no station was provided at the junction prior to the closure of the line to Newport, one was opened by the Isle of Wight Steam Railway in 1991 in order to provide a connection between the preserved railway and the Ryde to Shanklin line. *Phil Tatt/Online Transport Archive*

There was one intermediate station on the Bembridge branch; this was St Helens, which is pictured from the west as a train from Bembridge approaches. The Brading Harbour Improvement Railway & Works Co was authorised on 7 August 1874 to construct a line from St Helens, where it connected into the planned short freight-only branch serving Brading Harbour, to Bembridge along with improvements to the harbour itself. Financial problems and other difficulties meant that the line was not, however, opened from Bembridge to Brading until 27 May 1882. The line was operated from opening by the Isle of Wight Railway. From 1885 a train ferry service operated from Brading to Langstone on the Hayling Island branch; it incurred significant losses and was withdrawn three years later. The Brading Harbour Improvement Railway & Works Co became the Brading Harbour & Railway Co in 1896 and was transferred, by Act of Parliament dated 2 August 1898, to the Isle of Wight Railway. This view shows to good effect the junction for the short branch to the harbour, which was controlled by a signalbox, with the level crossing protecting the Bembridge to St Helens road. Brading harbour was, until the opening of Medina Quay in 1928, the primary commercial port serving the island. St Helens station closed with the branch on 21 September 1953 although the station building remains intact, having been converted into a private house.
Julian Thompson/Online Transport Archive

On 20 March 1953 No W15 *Cowes* awaits departure from Bembridge with a service towards Brading. Opened by the Brading Harbour Improvement Railway & Works Co on 27 May 1882, Bembridge station was provided with a single 220ft platform and run road loop as well as sidings for coal and general freight. The signalbox controlling the station was situated at the south end of the station under the platform canopy. The journey time for the 2¾-mile trip to Brading was about 10 minutes. No W15 was originally built at Nine Elms in December 1890 as LSWR No 195; it was destined to be third of the 'O2' class to be withdrawn on the island, being taken out of service in June 1956 and scrapped later the same year. The station at Bembridge was demolished in the early 1970s and a housing estate now occupies the site.
Julian Thompson/Online Transport Archive

There was one facet that made Bembridge unique amongst the various branch termini on the island in the post-war era and that was the provision of a turntable (Ventnor was originally constructed with one, but this was soon replaced with a simple crossing to access the run-round loop). The turntable was provided in order to save space at the somewhat constrained terminus; it could only turn locomotives with a maximum wheelbase of 30ft 11in. On 25 March 1950 No W14 *Fishbourne* is pictured making use of the facility. No W14 had originally been built at Nine Elms in July 1890 as LSWR No 178; being transferred to the Isle of Wight in 1936, No W14 was to achieve some 30 years of service on the island before withdrawal in January 1967. It was scrapped in May the same year.

Neil Davenport/Online Transport Archive

On 10 April 1954 No W17 *Seaview* is pictured just south of Brading with a southbound service heading towards Ventnor. Built as LSWR No 208 in December 1891, No W17 was transferred to the island in 1930. It was another of the class that survived through to the end of steam operation on the line from Ryde Pier Head at the end of December 1966.
Julian Thompson/Online Transport Archive

The 12.56pm service from Cowes to Sandown has got the road as it approaches its destination from the west on 20 March 1953. The first railway to reach Sandown was the Isle of Wight (Eastern Section) Railway, which was authorised on 23 July 1860 and opened from Ryde to Shanklin on 23 August 1864. The line from Sandown westwards was authorised as the Isle of Wight (Newport Junction) Railway on 31 July 1868. The new company was empowered to construct the 9½-mile line via Merstone with work finally commencing on 14 October 1870. However, due to problems in construction – and repeated failures to pass its Board of Trade inspection – it was not until 1 February 1875 that the line

opened from Sandown to Shide. The original station was enlarged during 1870 and 1871 in anticipation of the arrival of the Isle of Wight (Newport Junction) Railway. When recorded here the station still retained its freight facilities; these were, however, to be withdrawn on 15 November 1965. The Newport via Merstone line closed on 6 February 1956. Although Sandown station remains operational the trackbed of the closed line is now occupied by housing although, outside the town, the route is now a footpath and cycleway to Honningford and, effectively, Newport.
Julian Thompson/Online Transport Archive

In March 1950 W18 *Ningwood* is pictured in the down platform at Sandown with a service heading southbound towards Ventnor. Built as LSWR No 220 at Nine Elms in September 1891, the locomotive crossed the Solent in 1930. Withdrawn on 5 December 1965, No W18 was scrapped in January 1967.
Neil Davenport/Online Transport Archive

Viewed looking towards the north No W35 *Freshwater* is seen with a southbound service towards Ventnor at Sandown. No W35 was one of three of the class transferred to the island after World War 2. Built originally as LSWR No 181 at Nine Elms in 1890, the locomotive retained its original number under the SR before being renumbered 30181 by BR after Nationalisation. It was to survive until final withdrawal in October 1966. The box at Sandown, visible in the background, was unusual in that it was constructed on the platform and pierced the station awning; it was only through this location that the signalman could obtain good visibility of the layout of the curved station whilst also monitoring the Merstone line. The box was constructed by Saxby & Farmer and incorporated a 31-lever frame; it opened in 1893 and was officially closed on 30 October 1988. However, operational problems meant that it remained active until final closure on 25 March 1989.
F. E. J. Ward/Online Transport Archive

On 20 March 1953 No W21 *Sandown* is pictured one mile west of Shanklin with a service from Ryde St John's Road to Ventnor. Although the entire route from Ryde Pier Head was listed for closure in the *Reshaping Report* of March 1963, in the event only the section south of Shanklin was to be closed.
Julian Thompson/Online Transport Archive

The first intermediate station south of Shanklin en route to Ventnor was Wroxall and here No W22 *Brading* is pictured with a southbound service on 20 March 1953. Opened in November 1866, the station at Wroxall was initially provided with a single platform to the west – ie upside – of the line. A small goods yard was provided to the north of the Castle Road overbridge; the yard was to close on 5 October 1965. In 1925, in order to increase capacity on the route south of Shanklin, the Southern Railway installed a passing loop and second platform here – as illustrated in this view. The section of line south from Shanklin closed completely on 18 April 1966 and Wroxall station was subsequently demolished. The Station Hotel, visible above the up side platform shelter, is still extant, however, albeit now converted for residential use, as is the road overbridge.
Julian Thompson/Online Transport Archive

Viewed from the east, the constrained site of the station at Ventnor is all too apparent when seen from this angle as No W32 *Bonchurch* shunts a rake of coaches on 4 May 1958. Visible in the foreground is the substantial goods shed. The station was constructed in a working quarry and the space was extended as the railway's needs increased. The chambers constructed in the cliff face on the western side of the station site provided accommodation for a number of the merchants who made use of the goods yard.
Neil Davenport/Online Transport Archive

With the southern portal of the ¾-mile long Boniface Down Tunnel in the background, 'O2' No 20 *Shanklin* stands at the northern end of Ventnor station in 1955. Although the Isle of Wight (Eastern Section) Railway had opened as far as Shanklin on 23 August 1864, opposition from the Earl of Yarborough forced the railway to construct a deviation from the its original route and the section to Ventnor was not finally opened until 10 October 1866. *John McCann/Online Transport Archive*

Appropriately recorded at Ventnor, No W16 *Ventnor* stands in the station in September 1963 awaiting departure with a northbound service towards Ryde Pier Head. The locomotive was constructed at Nine Elms in June 1892 as LSWR No 217 and was transferred to the island in 1936. It was one of the locomotives that was to survive right through until the final withdrawal of steam-operated services, being officially withdrawn on 1 January 1967. *Phil Tatt/Online Transport Archive*

Viewed towards the north-west from one of the platforms, 'O2' No W19 *Osborne* stands in front of the quarry in March 1950. When the railway originally opened a temporary station was provided in what was still a working quarry. The original station was provided with a single platform, with two platform faces, two sidings, a run-round loop and a turntable. By the end of the 19th century the station and its facilities had been considerably expanded as a result of further excavation of the hillside in the background. No W19 was the second of the first 'O2s' to be transferred to the island in 1923. Built at Nine Elms in September 1891 as LSWR No 206, No W19 was to become the second of the island-based 'O2s' to be withdrawn – on 5 November 1955 – and was scrapped the following year.
Neil Davenport/Online Transport Archive

Viewed towards the buffer stops at Ventnor, one of the ex-LBSCR 0-6-0Ts runs round its train. When the station at Ventnor opened a short turntable – similar to that at Bembridge – was installed but this had been replaced by the end of the 19th century.

Viewed from the buffer stops at Ventnor, 'O2' No W18 *Ningwood* is seen receiving water in late 1955. The station was provided with three platform faces for passenger traffic with a fourth, on the extreme eastern side of the station, used for goods traffic and provided access to the substantial goods shed. The section of line from Shanklin to Ventnor was closed on 18 April 1966 and the station site was cleared in the early 1970s and redeveloped as a light industrial estate. The southern portal of the tunnel, however, remains extant as a reminder of the railway's presence in the town. *John McCann/Online Transport Archive*

In April 1946, 'Terrier' No W13 *Carisbrooke* is seen awaiting departure from Ventnor West with a service towards Merstone and Newport. No W13 had originally been built as LBSCR No 677

Wonersh at Brighton in July 1880.
Tony Wickens/Online Transport Archive

On 28 October 1948 No W13 *Carisbrooke* is seen again this time as it arrives at Ventnor West. The Newport, Godshill & St Lawrence Railway was authorised on 12 August 1889 to construct the six-mile branch from Merstone to Ventnor; it was not, however, until 20 July 1897 that the line opened as far as St Lawrence with the final section – to Ventnor – following on 1 June 1900. As such, the Ventnor section represented the last extension to the island's railway network. The terminus – known as Ventnor Town until it was renamed by the Southern Railway on 9 July 1923 – was not convenient and there were plans – never completed – to extend the line further towards the town centre. The original company went bankrupt in 1913 and its assets passed to the Isle of Wight Central Railway. By 1948 No W13 – one of only two of the class to operate on the island post-Nationalisation (the other being No 8 *Freshwater*, which was preserved following withdrawal) – was approaching the end of its career on the Isle of Wight; both it and No 8 were transferred back to the mainland in September 1949. Renumbered 32677 following its return to the mainland, the locomotive was finally withdrawn in September 1959 and scrapped at Eastleigh the following year.
John Meredith/Online Transport Archive

In March 1950 No W36 *Carisbrooke* stands in the platform at Ventnor West. Completed at Nine Elms in June 1891 as LSWR No 198, as BR No 30198 this was one of two 'O2s' transferred to the Isle of Wight in early 1949 – the other was No W35 *Freshwater* (the third post-war transfer – of No W34 Newport – had occurred in 1947) – and was to remain in service until June 1964. No W36 was scrapped in October 1965.
Neil Davenport/Online Transport Archive

With Newport station in the background, No W30 *Shorwell* departs northwards with the 5.5pm service to Cowes on 10 July 1955. The station was relocated and rebuilt as a through station in December 1875 following the final extension of the Isle of Wight (Newport Junction) Railway and the opening of the line from Smallbrook Junction. The new station included two through platforms, a loop creating an island platform for services to Ryde and Sandown, and a bay platform at the northern end of the platform for Cowes-bound services that was used primarily by services to and from Freshwater. Known briefly as Newport General from early 1876, it became Newport Central later that year; it lost its suffix in 1907. Built at Nine Elms in September 1892 as LSWR No 219, No W30 was transferred to the island in 1926; it was to achieve almost 40 years of service before final withdrawal in September 1965.
Julian Thompson/Online Transport Archive

On 8 April 1954 No W29 *Alverstone* enters Newport station with a service from Cowes to Sandown. Built at Nine Elms as LSWR No 202 in August 1891, No W29 was transferred to the island in 1926 and was to survive in service until May 1966. *Julian Thompson/Online Transport Archive*

Class O2 No W28 *Ashey* stands light engine at the southern end of Newport station. The station originally opened courtesy of the Cowes & Newport Railway on 16 June 1862 with a platform sited in the future goods yard. Newport station was finally to close to passenger services on 21 February 1966 with the final freight traffic ceasing on 18 April of the same year. Initially the station was the base of the Wight Locomotive Society but the group's occupation of the site ceased in January 1971 when the stock was moved to Havenstreet following purchase of the station site by the local council. Following this, the station was demolished and the site used to facilitate the construction of the Newport bypass.
F. E. J. Ward/Online Transport Archive

Shide station was the first south of Newport on the Isle of Wight Central Railway. Opened by the Isle of Wight (Newport Junction) Railway on 1 February 1875, Shide was to be the temporary terminus of the line until the extension was opened to Newport Pan Lane on 6 October 1875. The 9½-mile line from Sandown to Newport was authorised on 31 July 1868 but the railway was beset by financial problems almost from the start. The final link in the line from Pan Lane to form a connection with the Ryde & Newport Railway, which opened on 1 June 1879 (at which time Pan Lane station closed), was the final straw and the line became bankrupt. It was then operated under the aegis of the Official Receiver by the Cowes & Newport and Ryde & Newport railways until the creation of the Isle of Wight Central Railway on 1 July 1887. The line through Shide closed completely on 6 February 1956 with the withdrawal of services from the Newport to Sandown line via Merstone. This view, taken looking towards the south, shows to good effect the station's single platform and signalbox. After closure the station was demolished and the site is now occupied by a warehouse.

J. Joyce Collection/Online Transport Archive

In March 1950 No W32 *Bonchurch* is seen arriving at Merstone, junction for the line south to Ventnor West, with a service from Newport. The station at Merstone opened originally courtesy of the Isle of Wight (Newport Junction) Railway on 1 February 1875 and was provided with a single platform; it was rebuilt with an island platform in 1897 with the opening of the Newport, Godshill & St Lawrence Railway. With the opening of the Ventnor line, the station was renamed Merstone Junction; it lost the suffix on 1 October 1911. No W32 was built at Nine Elms as LSWR No 226 in November 1892 and was transferred to the island in 1928. It survived in service until October 1964 and was scrapped in October the following year.

Neil Davenport/Online Transport Archive

This view records the main building on the island platform at Merstone looking in the Newport direction. The junction for the line to Ventnor West was slightly to the south of the station as was the small signalbox. The station ceased to be a junction on 15 September 1952 when the Ventnor line closed. The Newport to Sandown via Merstone was to close completely on 6 February 1956.

By the early 1960s the station building had been demolished although the island platform remained. The site – with the still extant platform – is now the car park for the footpath and cycleway constructed on the erstwhile railway route.
Julian Thompson/Online Transport Archive

On 9 April 1954 a pick-up freight from Sandown approaches Merstone from the east behind 'E1' No W2 *Yarmouth*. This was one of four ex-LBSCR Class E1 0-6-0Ts based on the island post-war. Designed by Edward Stroudley, the first of the class were built in 1874 and, by 1891, when production ceased, a total of 80 had been completed. No W2 was originally LBSCR No 152 *Hungary* and was built at Brighton in October 1880. All four were transferred to the island in the early 1930s primarily for freight traffic; No W2 was the first of the quartet to be withdrawn, succumbing in October 1956. It was scrapped later the same year. Merstone had a small goods yard; this was to close contemporaneously with the withdrawal of passenger services over the line on 6 February 1956.
Julian Thompson/Online Transport Archive

On 19 March 1953 No W36 *Carisbrooke* approaches Horringford station with the 3.27pm service from Shanklin to Newport via Merstone. Problems with the construction of the Isle of Wight (Newport Junction) Railway meant that the line's planned opening was considerably delayed as the Board of Trade Inspectors found a number of issues that required resolution. This meant that normal – authorised – timetabled services did not commence from Shide to Sandown until 1 February 1875; however, for a brief period during 1872 a limited – and unauthorised – service was operated by the contractor. The station was provided with a single platform – as illustrated here – allied to a small goods yard located to the west; freight facilities were withdrawn on 6 February 1956, the same day as the line was closed completely. The station is still extant, having been converted into a private house, whilst the trackbed of the closed line to the east and west are now part of a footpath and cycleway.

Although the Freshwater, Yarmouth & Newport Railway was constructed to avoid as much heavy – and expensive – engineering as possible, there were a couple of significant structures along the route. One of these was the 576ft long trestle viaduct that allowed the railway to cross over the main Newport to Cowes road at Hunny Hill, Newport, which is seen here on 31 December 1949. The viaduct was demolished after the closure of the line. The construction of the 12-mile line to Freshwater was authorised on 26 August 1880 with construction eventually commencing in 1886. The first train operated on 10 August 1888 and the first freight traffic was carried on 1 September 1888 but it was not until 20 July 1889 that passenger services were introduced as the Board of Trade inspector required additional work, following his original inspection, before the latter could commence. Initially the line was worked by the Isle of Wight Central Railway but this arrangement ceased with the FY&NR assuming operation of the line on 1 July 1913. This forced the railway into bankruptcy and for the remainder of its independence until the Grouping in 1923 it was operated under the auspices of a manager appointed by the receivers.
John Meredith/Online Transport Archive

Although completed for the opening of the Freshwater, Yarmouth & Newport Railway on 20 July 1879, Watchingwell was originally a private station built for the use of Sir John Barrington Simeon, the MP for Southampton, for family and friends visiting his estate. It was not to appear in the public timetable until August 1923. The station, seen in this view from the west, was provided with a single platform; there were also limited freight facilities – a single 140ft long siding – but these were withdrawn in mid-1948. The station was downgraded to a halt at the same time and was closed completely when passenger services over the Freshwater line were withdrawn on 21 September 1953. The station building, now converted into a private house, and part of the platform are still extant.
F. E. J. Ward/Online Transport Archive

The next station west of Watchingwell Halt heading west towards Freshwater was officially Calbourne & Shalfleet although, as shown in this view of the station looking towards the west from the level crossing, only 'Calbourne' appears on the station nameboard. The station was modified by the Southern Railway after it took over the island's railway network at Grouping by the transfer of the corrugated iron and wooden ticket office from Newport following the closure of Freshwater, Yarmouth & Newport Railway's station in the town on 1 August 1923. The station had a single platform along with a short – 160ft long – siding for freight facilities. The station was to lose both is passenger services and freight facilities with the complete closure of the Freshwater line on 21 September 1953. Although the station building was subsequently demolished and a house built on the site, traces of the platform remain extant in the garden.

F. E. J. Ward/Online Transport Archive

On 17 March 1953 the 2.40pm service from Newport to Freshwater approaches Ningwood from the east. The photograph was taken from the road overbridge immediately to the east of the station itself.
Julian Thompson/Online Transport Archive

Two days later, on 19 March, 'O2' No W35 *Freshwater* is seen departing from Ningwood with the 12 noon service from Freshwater to Newport. The station opened for passenger services on 20 July 1889 and was to remain open until the final closure of the line on 21 September 1953. The station was provided with two platforms and the loop was extended by the Southern Railway after Grouping in order to accommodate longer trains. Following the line's closure, the station buildings were converted into a private house with the shelter on the up platform retained as a garden shed. The platforms are also still extant.
Julian Thompson/Online Transport Archive

Situated on the eastern shore of the Western Yar, Yarmouth's harbour was – and remains – one of the main entry points to the island with regular ferry services to and from Lymington – a fact recognised by the railway with the station nameboards advertising 'Alight here for slipway for boats to Lymington'. The reality was not quite that simple as there was a walk of almost a mile between the station and slipway through the town. The station – seen here looking from the north-west on 17 April 1949 – opened with the line to freight traffic on 10 August 1888 and to passenger services on 20 July 1889. It was originally provided with two platforms and a passing loop but the passing loop and westbound platform went out of use in the 1920s and were subsequently removed. The goods yard was situated on the northside of the line, to the east of the station, and is out of view to the left.

Neil Davenport/Online Transport Archive

On 17 August 1949 'O2' No W25 *Godshill* awaits departure from Yarmouth with a westbound service towards Freshwater. No W25 was built at Nine Elms as LSWR No 190; it was transferred to the island in 1925. It was withdrawn at the end of December 1962 and scrapped the following month. Yarmouth station closed completely with the withdrawal of services on the line between Newport and Freshwater on 21 September 1953. The station building survives and, during 2013 and 2014, underwent a major restoration. This work included an eastern extension, constructed to match the original building, with the station now accommodating a café. In addition to the building, the platform is also still extant although the signalbox is not original and is a modern replica designed to provide a hide for birdwatchers.
Neil Davenport/Online Transport Archive

The construction of the 12-mile long branch from Newport to Freshwater was a long draw out affair. The first company authorised – on 7 July 1873 – to build the line was dissolved on 23 July 1877; a second attempt was made three years later with authorisation given to the Freshwater, Yarmouth & Newport Railway on 26 July 1880 but it was not until 10 September 1888 that freight services commenced, with passenger services being introduced on 20 July 1889. Initially the line was operated by the Isle of Wight Central Railway but the Freshwater company took over operation itself on 1 January 1913. Never a great financial success, it did, however, retain its independence until Grouping in 1923. The station at Freshwater, viewed here from the east, was the largest on the line. It included a single platform, which was lengthened on several occasions to accommodate longer trains, as well as a small engine shed, which closed on 1 August 1923, and good facilities. The station closed completely with the withdrawal of freight and passenger services over the branch on 21 September 1953. The station was subsequently demolished and the site is now occupied by a supermarket.
F. E. J. Ward/Online Transport Archive

No W28 *Ashey* recorded awaiting departure with a service towards Newport from Freshwater. No W28 was new originally as LSWR No 186 when completed at Nine Elms in July 1890; it was transferred to the island in 1926 and was one of the type that survived to the

Recorded at Cowes on 23 June 1946 whilst still in South Railway ownership No W28 *Ashey* is seen again. The first railway to open on the Isle of Wight was the Cowes & Newport. The 4½-mile line was authorised on 8 August 1859 with work commencing on its construction on 15 October of the same year. Problems with construction allied to poor weather resulted in delay to the line's opening until 16 June 1862. At opening the line was operated by a contractor, Henry Martin, until 20 December 1875 when, following the opening of the Ryde & Newport Railway, a joint committee was established for the operation of the two lines. These and the Isle of Wight (Newport Junction) Railway were to merge on 1 July 1897 to create the Isle of Wight Central Railway.
Tony Wickens/Online Transport Arcchive

On 15 March 1953 an 'O2' is seen departing from Cowes with the 2.43pm service to Newport. The station was extended to three platforms as the island's railway network expanded but was to lose its passenger services with the withdrawal of the service via Newport to Ryde on 21 February 1966. It continued to handle freight traffic for a further few months, until freight facilities were withdrawn on 16 May 1966. The substantial stone and brick station building was demolished and the rest of the site cleared in the early 1970s. Used as a car park for some years, it has now been redeveloped as a supermarket.
Julian Thompson/Online Transport Archive

On 16 August 1953 No W34 *Newport* is seen entering Mill Hill, Cowes, station with a southbound service as the train emerges from the short tunnel that passed under the main Newport to Cowes road. Although the Cowes & Newport Railway opened on 16 June 1862 it was not until 1871 that the station at Mill Hill opened; it was slightly relocated nine years later. No W34 was one of the three locomotives transferred to the island post-war – in 1947 – and was originally LSWR No 201 when built at Nine Elms in July 1891. It was one of two locomotives withdrawn from service on the island in September 1955 – the other was No W23 *Totland* – and was scrapped later the same year. These were the first of their class to be withdrawn on the island. Mill Hill station closed with the line on 21 February 1966. The station building survived until demolition in the early 1970s and part of the site is now occupied by housing. The tunnel is still extant and traces of the former platform can still be seen where the former trackbed has been infilled.

Julian Thompson/Online Transport Archive

In February 1947 Class E4 0-6-2T No 2510 was transferred to the Isle of Wight for trials. The locomotive was not a success and was to return to the mainland in April 1949. It is seen here outside Newport shed on 28 October 1948, still bearing its original Southern livery and number, during its short sojourn on the island. The 'E4' class was designed by Billinton for the LBSCR, with the first of the type being completed at Brighton in December 1897. A total of 75 were completed, with the future No 2510 being delivered in December 1900. As BR No 32510 it was to survive in service until September 1962.

John Meredith/Online Transport Archive

Also on shed at Newport on 28 October 1948 was one of the four 'E1' class 0-6-0Ts class locomotives transferred to the island in the early 1930s. No W4 *Wroxall*, originally built as LBSCR No 131 *Gournay* at Brighton in November 1878, was modified at Ryde Works in October 1933; this improved the ride of the locomotive and the remaining three locomotives were also modified to improve their balance during 1935 and 1936. Primarily allocated to freight duties, the type was also used on passenger work but, as work diminished during the 1950s, the four locomotives were withdrawn as and when major overhauls were due. No 4 was the last of the four to be withdrawn, in October 1960, and was scrapped by the end of the year. One of the 80-strong class – No 110 *Burgundy* – was sold into industry in 1927 and rescued for preservation in the early 1960s. The locomotive was sold to the preserved Isle of Wight Steam Railway in 2012 and it is intended to be restored in the guise of one of the Isle of Wight-based engines – No W2 *Yarmouth*.
John Meredith/Online Transport Archive

In March 1950 No W3 *Ryde* is recorded outside St John's Road Works in its early British Railways livery. This ex-LBSCR Class E1 0-6-0T had originally No 154 *Madrid* when completed at Brighton Works in March 1881. This was the penultimate of the class to be withdrawn on the island, finally succumbing in June 1959; it was to be scrapped later in the year. *Neil Davenport/Online Transport Archive*

A month later, 'O2' No W33 *Bembridge* is on shed at Newport; this was one of three locomotives transferred to the island in 1936 (along with Nos W14 *Fishbourne* and W16 *Ventnor)* and was to remain in service until January 1967. Built at Nine Elms in August

In 1945 the railway network that served the
Isle of Wight was intact – less than a generation
later the majority of lines had closed and
steam traction had been replaced on the one
surviving section by surplus electric rolling
stock acquired from London Underground.

The railways on the Isle of Wight have always
attracted the enthusiast fraternity as, due to
their restricted loading gauge, they were
redolent of a much older era. Vintage rolling
stock hauled by diminutive locomotives were
the hallmarks of the railway down the years
until the final withdrawal of steam. Featuring
a wide range of images from the two decades
of operation after the end of World War 2
Steam on the Isle of Wight: The Postwar Years is
an evocative reminder of the railways that
once served the island.

£9.99

UNIQUE BOOKS

www.uniquebooks.pub

ISBN 978-0-9957493-9-9

9 780995 749399

BUILDING THE BRIDGE

LILLIAN KING